JOB MATTERS

GASTRONOMIE-BERUFE

Neil Deane

VER*I*TAS

Cornelsen

Contents

Unit	1	Greetings	4
Unit	2	The hotel workers	6
Unit	3	Hotel facilities	8
Unit	4	Hotel reservations	10
Unit	5	Confirmations	12
Unit	6	Dealing with complaints	14
Unit	7	Ordering and asking for things	16
Unit	8	Breakfast	18
Unit	9	Lunchtime	20
Unit	10	British tea tradition	22
Unit	11	Dinner	24
Unit	12	Can we have the bill, please?	26
Unit	13	The world of food	28
Unit	14	Food specialities	30
Unit	15	The tools of the kitchen and restaurant	32
Unit	16	The chef	34
Unit	17	Fish and shellfish	36
Unit	18	Are you a vegetarian?	38
Unit	19	Having a drink	40
Unit	20	Commercial catering	42

Reference

	Technical wordlist	44
	Conversion tables	48

UNIT 1

Greetings

1 A reservation

a) Daniel works at the "Bauernstübl" restaurant and is speaking to a guest on the telephone. Read the conversation and fill in the information in Daniel's reservation notes.

Daniel: Good evening. How can I help you?
Guest: I'd like to reserve a table for two, please.
Daniel: Yes, certainly. When would you like the reservation for?
Guest: Tomorrow evening at about 7 o'clock.
Daniel: Let me have a look in our reservation book.
So, that's Friday, 15 April at 7 o'clock.
I'm sorry, we have nothing free at 7. Would 8 o'clock be OK?
Guest: Yes, that's OK.
Daniel: Could I have your name please?
Guest: Yes. Gary Watkins.
Daniel: Could you spell your surname please?
Guest: Yes, that's W-A-T-K-I-N-S.
Daniel: Thank you. I just have one more question. Are you a smoker or non-smoker?
Guest: I'm a non-smoker.
Daniel: OK, I'll put you in the non-smoking part of the restaurant, Mr Watkins.
We look forward to seeing you on Friday then.
Guest: Thank you, bye.
Daniel: Bye.

RESERVATION NOTES:
Name of guest: _____
Date: _____
Time: _____
Number of persons: _____
Smoker/Non-smoker? _____

b) Find the English equivalents in the dialogue and write them next to the German.

1 Wie kann ich Ihnen helfen? _____

2 Morgen Abend _____

3 Können Sie Ihren Familiennamen buchstabieren?
_____

4 Um 7 Uhr haben wir nichts frei. _____

5 Wäre 8 Uhr in Ordnung? _____

6 Bis Freitag! _____

UNIT 1

2 Checking in at a hotel

Look at these 10 sentences. Who says what? (Write down the numbers.)

1 Welcome to our hotel.
2 Do you take credit cards?
3 What time is breakfast?
4 Shall we give you a wake-up call?
5 The breakfast room is on the left.
6 When is lunch?
7 Have you enjoyed your stay with us?
8 I would like to check out.
9 Can I have your passport, please?
10 Is this your luggage?

The guest says: _____   The receptionist says: _____

3 Which words?

Put the following words into the gaps in this small talk conversation at the hotel reception.

> chambermaid • key card • reserve • food • receipt • departure • passport • stay • ready for a holiday • view

Daniel: Oh, hello Mr Jenkins. How are you?

Guest: I'm very well. I was really (1) _____ . How are you?

Daniel: I'm busy, but fine! When is your day of (2) _____ , Mr Jenkins?

Guest: Oh, I'm leaving tomorrow.

Daniel: I hope you have enjoyed your (3) _____ with us.

Guest: Oh, yes. The service, (4) the _____ , the rooms, and the atmosphere were all very good. I'm coming back next year.

Daniel: Good! Shall I (5) _____ a room for you?

Guest: Yes, that's a good idea. Could I have a room with a (6) _____ of the sea next time? Could I also have a (7) _____ for this week?

Daniel: Yes, of course. Oh by the way, did you find your (8) _____ ?

Guest: Yes. I had put it inside my (9) _____ ! It was the (10) _____ who suggested that I check my passport and tickets. It was good advice!

Daniel: Well, I'm glad that everything is fine now. See you tomorrow.

4 Small talk

Practise with a partner.

Hotel Reception:
Good morning, Mr/Mrs …   Did you sleep well?
How are you today?   Can I help you?

Guest:
I'm having a bit of a problem with the/my … .
I need a/some … .
Have you got …?

5

UNIT 2

The hotel workers

1 My job

Listen to six people talking about what they do at their hotel and match their jobs on the left to the duties on the right.

1 Jim, the porter,
2 Linda, the receptionist,
3 Julia, the sous-chef,
4 Robert, the pastry chef,
5 Mary, the housekeeper,
6 Alfonso, the head chef,

a) handles all the reservations.
b) helps guests when they need a taxi.
c) bakes all the bread and prepares the hot desserts.
d) prepares all the soups and hot starters.
e) writes the menu and is responsible for the main courses.
f) helps guests when they want dry cleaning and laundry services.

2 Jobs and words

a) When you see these words which jobs do you think about?

Word	Job
Ice cubes	_____
Pots	_____
Notepad	_____
Staff meetings	_____
Laundry	_____
Bills	_____
Cases	_____

b) Write the English names for these things under the pictures.

3 Who says what?

Here are 10 typical things you will hear spoken by hotel and catering staff. Who says what? Match the following jobs and the sentences.

> doorman • housekeeper • hotel manager • pastry chef • porter • receptionist • waiter/waitress

1. _____ : I'll get you a clean spoon straight away.
2. _____ : Could you sign the registration form at the bottom, please?
3. _____ : When would you like your laundry to be ready, sir?
4. _____ : Do the guests at table three want cream with their cakes?
5. _____ : Did you have anything out of the mini bar?
6. _____ : Which room shall I take your cases to?
7. _____ : I'm afraid the mushroom soup isn't on the menu today.
8. _____ : I need your holiday application forms by the end of the month.
9. _____ : Would you like a taxi?
10. _____ : Are you ready to order now?

4 Complaints

a) Work with a partner.
Which lists do these words fit into?
(Some words fit into more than one list.)

> blunt • chipped • cold • corked • dirty • greasy • missing • overdone • salty • too dry • too sweet • tough • underdone

SOUP	STEAK	WINE	KNIFE	GLASS
____	____	____	____	____
____	____	____	____	____
____	____	____	____	____
____	____	____	____	____

b) Practise with a partner.

Waiter/Waitress: Is something wrong?

Guest: Yes. This soup is too salty.

Waiter/Waitress: I'll …
 take it back.
 bring you another …
 tell the chef to …
 …

Guest: Yes. There is a hair in my …

Guest: Yes. My … is …

UNIT 3

Hotel facilities

1 What types of rooms are there?

Match the words and the symbols.

1 Single room
2 Honeymoon suite
3 Double room
4 Suite
5 Twin room

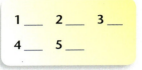

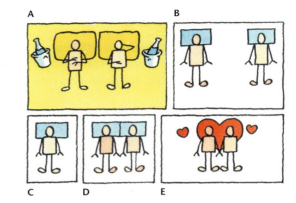

T3 2 What do guests want from your hotel?

Match the guests below with the facilities they might need in your hotel. Put the number of the facility in the brackets next to the guest and check the answers A–G by listening to the CD. (H and I aren't on the audio text.)

Guests

A A businessman from the USA.   (_____)

B A husband and wife with two small girls under five.   (_____)

C A businesswoman who doesn't have a car but needs   (_____)
   to be mobile in the evenings.

D The leader of an excursion.   (_____)

E A husband and wife with baby twins.   (_____)

F A disabled person.   (_____)

G The organizer of a football team excursion.   (_____)

H A Las Vegas gambler with two girlfriends.   (_____)

I A family with three children, 5, 7 and 14 years old.   (_____)
   The 7 year-old is in a wheelchair.

FACILITIES

1 Babysitting service
2 Chauffeur service
3 Games room
4 24-hour room service
5 Disabled access
6 Video conferencing
7 Nappy-changing table

BE = nappy
AE = diaper

UNIT 3

3 Which facilities?

Listen to the dialogue on the CD and list the facilities and services the hotel can provide for Sarah Faulkner's conference. Then name two things it can't provide.

Things it **can** provide:

1 _____
2 _____
3 _____
4 _____
5 _____
6 _____

Things it **can't** provide:

1 _____
  _____
2 _____
  _____

4 What's missing?

Sometimes hotel staff forget to put something in the room or guests want something extra. Complete the words in this list:

1 An extra _____
2 Some _____
3 A _____
4 A _____
5 Another _____
6 An extra _____
7 An _____
8 Another _____

5 Things in your hotel room

Match the English words on the left with the German words on the right.

1	shampoo	A	Fernbedienung	1 ___
2	bath	B	Aschenbecher, Ascher	2 ___
3	remote control	C	Spiegel	3 ___
4	curtains	D	Papierkorb	4 ___
5	ashtray	E	Duschschlauch	5 ___
6	air conditioning	F	Haarwaschmittel	6 ___
7	wastepaper bin	G	Kleiderbügel	7 ___
8	shower hose	H	Gardinen, Vorhänge	8 ___
9	coat hanger	I	Badewanne	9 ___
10	mirror	J	Klimaanlage	10 ___

9

UNIT 4

Hotel reservations

1 Specialist language for reservations

Read this confirmation of a hotel reservation and think of what other words could replace the words underlined in the confirmation. Then choose the most suitable replacement word from the list below and underline it.

CONFIRMATION

Dear Sir or Madam,

Your web reservation number: 564098

Your arrival date: 23/9/05 12.00
5 Number of nights: 2
<u>Anticipated</u> (**1**) date of departure: 25/9/05

We are pleased to confirm your requested <u>reservation</u> (**2**) in the following hotel:
Hotel Queens, Manchester, GB. You <u>selected</u> (**3**) the rooms below:
Type of room: 1 x single at £95.00 per overnight stay.

10 To <u>finalize</u> (**4**) your reservation the hotel requires a credit card number within 3 days. Please give your name, credit card number and expiry date. If we do not receive this information, we cannot <u>ensure</u> (**5**) the availability of the room quoted above.

Please send us this information as soon as possible by letter, fax or by using the clients' control panel on our website. Please rest assured that the online credit card payment
15 process is completely secure. (See the secure lock symbol at the bottom of your screen.)

If you wish to cancel your reservation, we would be grateful for an early reply to this e-mail. We hope you have a pleasant <u>trip</u> (**6**) and look forward to welcoming you when you arrive in Manchester.

Best <u>wishes</u> (**7**),
20 Best Hotels Europe

1 expected • targeted • delayed • postponed

2 order • demand • booking • time share

3 agreed • made • chose • reviewed

4 confirm • deadline • cancel • renew

5 take • guarantee • move • make

6 voyage • journey • stay • move

7 regards • greetings • hellos • times

10

UNIT 4

2 Finding the right expressions

Read through the following expressions from letters which hotels send to guests and match the English and German equivalents.

1 Leider haben wir keine Einzelzimmer.
2 Wir mussten Ihre Reservierung stornieren.
3 Mit den besten Wünschen
4 Wir freuen uns auf Ihre Bestätigung.
5 Können Sie uns Ihren Anreisetag bestätigen?
6 Wir freuen uns darauf, Sie zu begrüßen.
7 Bezüglich Ihrer Reservierung …

A We had to cancel your reservation.
B We look forward to your confirmation.
C Concerning your reservation …
D Can you confirm your date of arrival?
E Unfortunately we have no single rooms.
F Best wishes
G We look forward to welcoming you.

1 ___ , 2 ___ , 3 ___ , 4 ___ , 5 ___ , 6 ___ , 7 ___

3 Voicemail reservation

Listen to the voicemail message and then put the following sentences in the correct order.

A Could you confirm my reservation by phone?
B My mobile number is 0170 366 581.
C Hello, my name is Tom Jenkins.
D Thank you. Bye.
E Could you also reserve a table for dinner at 7.30 p.m. on the 14th, please?
F We are arriving in Graz at 6.00 p.m. on the 14th of June and we are staying until the 18th.
G I would like to reserve a double room for my wife and myself.

1 ___ , 2 ___ , 3 ___ , 4 ___ , 5 ___ , 6 ___ , 7 ___

4 Storing reservation information

Enter the information from the guest in the exercise above into the gaps on the hotel's computer program. (Write dates like this: Day/Month/Year.)

GUEST PROFILE

Surname:		First name:	
Country:	Great Britain	Telephone:	

RESERVATION

Arrival:		Thursday	Remarks:
Departure:		Monday	
Nights:		Room: 0733	
Adults:		Room type:	

11

UNIT 5

Confirmations

1 Mixed-up e-mail

The hotel's computer is leaving out the vowels! Write in the missing vowels.

Hotel WINGATE

Dear Mr Metcalf

We are (1) d __ l __ ght __ d that you enjoyed your recent (2) p __ ck __ g __ holiday with us. We are also pleased that you have decided to make a (3) r __ p __ __ t booking at our hotel. We have reserved the following room for you: a (4) n __ n-sm __ k __ ng room at 33 Euro per day (5) __ ncl __ d __ ng breakfast from 2nd till 8th June.

At the weekend breakfast is (6) s __ rv __ d until 12.00 as a buffet and on Saturday we have a (7) b __ nq __ __ t dinner which is included in the total price.

If you require any additional (8) m __ __ ls, for example, a light lunch or evening snacks, we can offer you this at a 25% (9) d __ sc __ __ nt on the normal restaurant prices during your stay with us.

Best wishes

Emma Hitchins (Manager)

HOTEL WINGATE • DODDERINGTON • BERKS BN13 6PQ • TEL. (0044) 1740 656 831

2 Who said what?

Look at these expressions taken from a telephone conversation between a guest and a receptionist at a hotel. Who said what?
Tick (✔) the correct person.

		Guest	Receptionist
1	Yes, the price includes value added tax.	☐	☐
2	When will you be arriving?	☐	☐
3	Could you give me directions to the hotel?	☐	☐
4	I'm sorry you haven't received our confirmation yet.	☐	☐
5	I'd like the largest room you have.	☐	☐
6	I'm sorry, but we don't have facilities for pets.	☐	☐
7	I don't think I'll be arriving before midnight.	☐	☐
8	Could you confirm your booking in writing, please?	☐	☐

UNIT 5

3 Telephone problems?

Here are some useful expressions when talking to customers on the phone.
Match the German expressions with the equivalent English expressions.

1 Wie bitte?
2 Können Sie das bitte wiederholen?
3 Wie kann ich Ihnen helfen?
4 Also, darf ich das noch einmal vorlesen?
5 Wann ist Ihr Ankunftstag?
6 Benötigen Sie einen Parkplatz?
7 Wie möchten Sie bezahlen?
8 Sollen wir Ihnen eine Bestätigung schicken?
9 Brauchen Sie eine Wegbeschreibung?
10 Ja, wir haben Nichtraucherzimmer.

A What's your date of arrival?
B How would you like to pay?
C Yes, we have no-smoking rooms.
D How can I help you?
E Pardon?
F Can you repeat that, please?
G Do you need directions?
H Do you need a parking space?
I So, may I read that back to you?
J Should we send you a confirmation?

1 ___ , 2 ___ , 3 ___ , 4 ___ , 5 ___ , 6 ___ , 7 ___ , 8 ___ , 9 ___ , 10 ___

4 Role play: a telephone call

Work with a partner. One of you is Mr/Mrs Green. The other is the hotel receptionist.
If you are Mr/Mrs Green, you are telephoning to make or confirm a booking.
Before you call the hotel, you should have the most important information ready.
The best way to do this is to make some notes:

How long? _____

Date of arrival? _____

Number of people? _____

What type of room(s)? _____

B+B or half board? _____

If you are the receptionist, you are taking a telephone call from a guest who is making or confirming a booking. Before the guest calls, think about the questions he or she may ask. What questions do you need to ask? What information do you need to give the guest? Make some notes before you start the telephone call with your partner. For example:

Time of arrival?
Rooms are not available until after …
Breakfast/Lunch/… is served at …
The restaurant/bar/… closes at …
Payment: cash/credit card/in advance/address for bill/…?
The swimming pool/sauna/… opens at …
W-LAN available?
Garage?

UNIT 6

Dealing with complaints

1 What would you say?

Guests say the following things to you. Choose the best reply.

1 My remote control isn't working.
2 There is no complimentary drink in my room.
3 I can't get any hot water from the shower.
4 Excuse me, but my soup isn't really hot.
5 I think you've made a mistake in my booking.
6 I ordered a "Jungle Breeze", not a "Bloody Mary".
7 I can't find the switch for the heating in my room.
8 I ordered a sandwich half an hour ago and I'm still waiting!
9 The people in the next room are keeping me awake.
10 I'm not happy with the way my room has been cleaned.

Your reply?

A I'll call them immediately and ask them to be quiet. Which side is the noise coming from?
B The batteries are probably flat. I'll have some sent up immediately.
C Let me have a look. You're right. I'll change it at once.
D Oh I'm sorry, sir/madam. I'll mix you a "Jungle Breeze" straight away.
E Oh, sorry. I'll have it warmed up for you.
F I'll speak to the housekeeper and she'll send somebody up. Please accept my apologies.
G Try turning the red handle to the right.
H It's behind the curtain, near the TV.
I I'm very sorry. I'll speak to the kitchen about it. Can you give us ten minutes?
J Have you looked in the fridge? It's normally in there.

1 ___ , 2 ___ , 3 ___ , 4 ___ , 5 ___ , 6 ___ , 7 ___ , 8 ___ , 9 ___ , 10 ___

2 Double check

Look through A–J again and find the English for the following expressions:

1 Es tut mir leid. = _____

2 Ich lasse sofort welche hochschicken. = _____

3 Ich spreche mit ... = _____

4 Ich bitte Sie um Verständnis. = _____

5 Ich rufe sie sofort an. = _____

6 Ich ändere es gleich. = _____

7 Ich lasse es für Sie aufwärmen. = _____

3 Bad news in the hotel

Look at the pictures and complete the sentences.

1 He'll be late because they have forgotten his w_____ u_____ c_____ !
2 It's too hot because the a_____ c_____ is out of order.
3 She can't check in yet because the room hasn't been t_____ u_____ .
4 I think you've made a mistake, Miss. This b_____ can't be right!
5 Help! Help! I'm s_____ in the lift! Please get me out of here!

4 Role play: hotel humour

Act short sketches with a partner.

Guest:	Night porter:
This is Mr/Ms/Mrs … in room …	Hello. How can I help you?
I'm tired of life! I'm going to jump out of the window.	• Very well, but you must pay your bill first. • Your room is on the ground floor. • Use a window at the front of the hotel. The view is better.
There's a ghost in my room! It's horrible!	• Really? Then I must charge you for a double room. • Guests aren't allowed to have visitors in their rooms after ten o'clock. • That isn't a ghost. It's the chambermaid.
Please bring us a bottle of champagne and two glasses.	• I'll send you three glasses because your wife/husband is on the way to your room.

Can you think of any more?

UNIT 7

Ordering and asking for things

1 What would you say?

Choose suitable answers from the box and write them in the gaps provided:

> here you are • keen on • I'd like • what about •
> I'd prefer • I'm afraid • how can I help you •
> I'll have • certainly • can I have

Waiter: Good evening, sir. _____ (1)?

Guest: _____ (2) the menu, please?

Waiter: Yes, of course, _____ (3). Would you like to order a drink?

Guest: Yes, please. What is the house white?

Waiter: We've got a Sauvignon blanc and an excellent Chardonnay.

Guest: In that case, a glass of Chardonnay, please.

Waiter: _____ (4), sir.

Waiter: Here's your wine. Are you ready to order?

Guest: Yes, _____ (5) a salad as a starter, please.

Waiter: Yes, and what would you like as a main dish?

Guest: I'd like fish, please. I'll have the salmon.

Waiter: I'm sorry, but _____ (6) the salmon is sold out. _____ (7) steak? The steak is excellent today.

Guest: No, I'm not too _____ (8) red meat. _____ (9) the chicken curry.

Waiter: With rice or nan bread?

Guest: _____ (10) rice. Oh, and could you bring me some mineral water please?

Waiter: Yes, of course. Still or sparkling?

Guest: Still, please.

2 Role play: mini-dialogues

Work with a partner.

GUEST:
I'd like …   wine list/bill/…
Could you …?   English mustard/vinegar/…
Can I …?   glass/plate/…
Have you got …?   knife/fork/…
Please bring me …   clean/extra/…
Is/Are the …?   fresh/local/salted/…

WAITER/WAITRESS:
I don't know. I must ask the …
I'm afraid, we haven't/don't …
Of course. I'll bring it/them/…
Certainly. It won't take a minute.
That will be extra.
I'm sorry, but …

16

3 What would you say?

In each group choose the question you think is the most polite. Use a 'tick' (✔).

A 1 Would you like wine with your meal?
  2 We have wine. Do you want some?
  3 Will you have wine, beer or nothing?

B 1 Any problems?
  2 Is everything OK?
  3 Is your meal in order?

C 1 What else do you want?
  2 Would you like anything else?
  3 Anything else?

D 1 Was your meal good?
  2 Did the meat taste OK?
  3 Was everything to your satisfaction?

E 1 Fancy a dessert?
  2 How about something else?
  3 Can I bring you anything else?
     A coffee, a brandy or a dessert?

4 Explaining something on the menu.

a) Explaining Austrian or German dishes to tourists isn't easy. Can you complete these descriptions?

> small, spicy sausages • potato dumplings • cabbage, but pickled in brine • cider • stew

1 What exactly is 'Sauerkraut'? – Well, it's rather like _____

2 What are 'Kartoffelknödel'? – They are similar to _____

3 What are 'Nürnberger Bratwürste'? – They are _____

4 What is 'Eintopf'? – It's a kind of _____

5 What is 'Apfelwein'? – It tastes a bit like _____

b) Work with a partner.

> Excuse me. What is …?

> Well, …

UNIT 8

Breakfast

1 Hotel breakfasts in Britain

Work with a partner. Together decide what you would expect to get for breakfast in a good British hotel and put them in a list. Then put the food and drinks into categories like this:

DRINKS:

hot	cold
___	___
___	___
___	___
___	___
___	___
___	___

FOOD:

hot	cold
___	___
___	___
___	___
___	___
___	___
___	___

2 What's for breakfast?

Work with a partner.
Look at this photo of a breakfast buffet in an English hotel. How many things can you name?

UNIT 8

3 English or Viennese breakfast?

First match the adjectives to the nouns.
Then decide whether these breakfast dishes are part of a typical English or Viennese breakfast.
(Some things can go into both lists.)

ADJECTIVES	NOUNS
1 wholemeal	tomato
2 grilled	pastries
3 black	jam
4 Danish	kippers
5 Scottish	beans
6 baked	pudding
7 cold	rolls
8 strawberry	cuts
9 crispy	bread

English breakfast:
_____
_____
_____
_____
_____
_____
_____
_____

Viennese breakfast:
_____
_____
_____
_____
_____
_____
_____
_____

4 Word search: laying the table

Look at the word search on the right.
There are 14 words connected with items you put on a breakfast table.
They go across ➡ and down ⬇.
Find them and circle them in the box.
Then write the words in your exercise book.

K	X	S	P	O	O	N	S	S	A	S	W	S
N	C	U	T	L	E	R	Y	A	E	U	S	E
I	G	L	A	S	S	E	S	L	O	G	G	R
F	O	R	K	L	A	S	H	T	R	A	Y	V
E	Y	K	B	C	U	P	V	X	N	R	H	I
T	A	B	L	E	C	L	O	T	H	D	C	E
M	P	L	A	T	E	Z	U	E	I	L	Y	T
P	E	P	P	E	R	U	I	L	D	P	J	T
M	R	P	Y	D	F	H	J	W	A	C	B	E

19

UNIT 9

Lunchtime

1 Is there a set menu?

A businessman comes in for lunch. Here are some of the phrases he and the waiter use. Who says what? Write down the letters of the phrases.

A   Is there a set menu?
B   Would you like to order your drinks now?
C   Are you ready to order now?
D   Could I have a salad instead of potatoes?
E   You can choose any of the pasta dishes numbered 1–6. They are in the set menu offer.
F   Yes, coffee is included.
G   I'm afraid those prices are only valid from 12.00 p.m. to 3.00 p.m.
H   Do I get a reduction if I don't have a dessert?
I   Yes, that was very tasty.
J   I can recommend the Chardonnay; it goes very well with the chicken.

Guest says:
_____

Waiter says:
_____

2 Lunchtime variations

Hotels, bars, pubs and restaurants offer different types of food and service at lunchtime. You are talking to a guest. Explain the different possibilities on the left by choosing an appropriate explanation on the right.

1   All you can eat
2   Self-service
3   Finger food
4   A sit-down meal
5   Bar snacks
6   Take-away facilities
7   Sandwiches freshly cut

A   You are seated at a table and the food is served.
B   We can pack any food on offer for you to take away.
C   You choose the filling and we make the sandwich.
D   You have to go to the bar and order food yourself.
E   Snacks you can eat without using a knife and fork.
F   You can eat as much as you like of a dish at a fixed price.
G   Things like sandwiches, baguettes and small meals.

Which pub would you choose if you were

a) a vegetarian?

_____
_____

b) a non-smoker?

_____
_____

UNIT 9

3 Explaining signs

Some foreign guests can't understand the signs in and around your restaurant or hotel. Can you help them? Choose the correct translation from the sentences below the pictures.

A We are not responsible for items left in our cloakroom.
B Free beer tomorrow!
C Our lunchtime menu is only available on weekdays between 12.00 p.m. and 3.00 p.m.
D All meals are also available for take-away.
E If you enjoyed it here, tell your friends. If you didn't, tell us!

1 ___ , 2 ___ , 3 ___ , 4 ___ , 5 ___

4 Can I help you?

Look at the answers. What were the questions?

WAITER/WAITRESS: GUEST:

1 _____ ? – No, just one person.
2 _____ ? – Yes, it was very nice thanks.
3 _____ ? – Not quite. Can you give me two minutes?
4 _____ ? – No, just the main course.
5 _____ ? – No, I'll have the bill, please.

21

British tea tradition

1 Why is tea so popular in Britain?

Read the text and answer the questions below.

Tea first became popular in China. The British liked it and took tea plants to their biggest colony, India. People in Britain began to drink tea because it was so cheap and it was very easy to make.

5 Today people in Britain drink tea every day and sometimes drink ten cups a day! But the British don't normally drink many different kinds of tea – the most popular type is black tea, normally served with milk and/or sugar. Austrians, for example, often drink different fruit teas, normally without milk and sugar.

Austrians and Germans often eat cakes with their coffee, whereas the British usually prefer
10 biscuits. Tea is drunk at all times of the day and with all types of meals: breakfast, lunch and evening meal. A cup of tea can be drunk with everything and, as they say in Britain: "There's nothing like a nice cup of tea!" When you are visiting a family in Britain, you shouldn't say "No" to a cup of tea – it's the time of the day when people relax and find time to talk to each other.

1 Which type of tea is more popular in Austria?

_____

2 Why did the British start drinking tea?

_____

3 Where did tea first come from?

_____

4 Why shouldn't you say "No" to a cup of tea?

_____

2 Teatime British style

a) Work with a partner and act this dialogue. What are the missing words?

> fresh • brown • white • black • boiling • cooking • condensed • evaporated

WAITRESS:
Is there a problem with the tea?
It's our special fruit tea. Don't you like it?
Oh, you mean (**1**) … tea!
I'll bring you some immediately.
Yes, of course. What sort of milk?
Do you mean (**3**) … milk?

Yes, certainly.

BRITISH COUPLE:
Well, it has a strange taste.
Not really. We would just like normal tea.
Well, yes. I think so.
Could you also bring some milk, please?
Well, normal milk. Not this (**2**) … milk.
Yes, please. Oh, and there's one more thing.
Could you make sure that the water is (**4**) …?

UNIT 10

b) Now complete the three golden rules for serving British tea.

1 Always serve _____ water.

   Hot water isn't good enough!

2 Never serve _____

   milk. It must be fresh milk, of course!

3 The British prefer _____ tea.

   It can be either tea leaves or tea bags,

   but it must be quite strong!

3 Problems

In all of the following dialogues a problem is being discussed.
Listen to these brief dialogues in a restaurant and fill in the missing words.

> bitter • cold • herbal • missing • sour • weak

1 I'm afraid this coffee is rather _____

2 I'm _____ a coffee spoon.

3 This milk is _____

4 That's _____ tea.

5 This tea is too _____.

6 This coffee is nearly _____.

4 Asking questions

Look at the answers. What are the questions?

1 _____ with your tea/coffee?

   – Yes, please. Brown sugar would be nice.

2 _____ with your coffee?

   – No, no cake thanks. Just coffee.

3 _____ our cakes?

   – No, I haven't. I think I'll try one.

4 _____ our speciality "Melange"?

   – Yes, it's very tasty.

5 _____ similar to English coffee?

   – No, it's very different to English coffee. Your coffee is much stronger.

23

UNIT 11

Dinner

1 Definitions

**a) Match the cooking verbs on the left with the correct definition.
Write the correct letter next to the numbers below:**

1	boil	A	Place food over boiling water so it cooks in the steam.
2	steam	B	Cook strips of vegetables or meat quickly by stirring them in hot oil.
3	fry	C	Heat something to the point where it forms bubbles.
4	roast	D	Cook food in hot fat or oil.
5	stir-fry	E	Cook bread, cakes, potatoes, etc. in an oven.
6	grill	F	Fry food quickly in a little hot fat.
7	sauté	G	Cook food under or over a very strong heat.
8	bake	H	Cook meat, without liquid in an oven or over a fire.
9	simmer	I	Cook food in water that is just under boiling point.

1 ___ , 2 ___ , 3 ___ , 4 ___ , 5 ___ , 6 ___ , 7 ___ , 8 ___ , 9 ___

**b) Read the two definitions and then
put the following words into two lists.**

Besides salt, herbs (the fresh or dried leaves of a plant) and spices (a dry powder made from either the plant or its seed) are the main ways of adding flavour to food.

cinnamon • chives • cloves •
cumin • ginger • mint •
nutmeg • parsley •
pepper • rosemary • thyme

HERBS:
_____
_____
_____
_____
_____
_____

SPICES:
_____
_____
_____
_____
_____
_____

2 How would you say it?

a) Translate the following food items into English:

1 Bratkartoffeln _____ 2 Spiegeleier _____

3 Püree _____ 4 Reis _____

5 Rühreier _____ 6 Pommes frites _____

**b) Describe your favourite dish in English. Does it have an English name?
If not, can you think of something suitable?**

UNIT 11

3 What does a salad consist of?

a) Which ingredients could go into a fruit salad and a fresh salad? Put the following words under the right headings.
(Some can go into both, of course.)

onion • grapes • apple • herbs •
banana • lettuce • cherries • lemon •
radish • spring onions • melon •
red/green peppers •
garlic • salt • pepper • oil •
vinegar • sugar • honey • mustard

FRUIT SALAD:
_____
_____
_____
_____
_____
_____

FRESH SALAD:
_____
_____
_____
_____
_____
_____

4 Find the odd-one-out

Underline the word which does not fit.

1 **flour:** oil, pie, cake, roll
2 **soup:** salt, pepper, chocolate, spices
3 **milk:** butter, cheese, cream, egg
4 **dinner:** roast beef, sugar, soup, raspberry tart
5 **cake:** flour, salad, butter, eggs

5 Role play: describing food

Work with a partner. Try and use the words you learned in the other exercises in this unit.

Can you tell me what a "pizza tonno" is, please?

Yes, certainly, Sir/Madam.

Guest:
lasagne
potato soup
Wiener Schnitzel
Tafelspitz
apple pie
Kaiserschmarren

Waiter/Waitress:
It consists of …
It is made from/with …
It is eaten with …
It is served with …
In English it is called …

Can you describe any other dishes in English?

UNIT 12

Can we have the bill, please?

1 Payment – words that go together

> advance • the meal • the bill • receipt • 49 Euros • credit cards • transfer • credit card

Complete the sentences with the words in the box.

1 That was a wonderful meal. We'd like to pay _____ now, please.
2 Do you need a special _____ for the Inland Revenue*?
3 Do you accept _____ ?
4 I normally pay cash but I'll pay by _____ today.
5 That comes to _____ .
6 He was very kind and he paid for _____ .
7 Can I pay the hotel bill by bank _____ ?
8 We have to pay for the sightseeing tour in _____ .

* *Finanzamt*

2 Role play: checking out

Work with a partner. The guest is checking out. Try and use some of the words you practised above with the following phrases:

- I'd like to …
- Would you ….?
- Can I ….?
- Do you ….?
- I'd like …
- That …
- I need …

GUEST:	RECEPTIONIST:
Sie möchten auschecken und zahlen.	Sie fragen den Gast nach der Zahlungsart.
Sie fragen, ob sie Kreditkarten akzeptieren.	Sie bejahen. Sie teilen den zu zahlenden Betrag mit.
Sie legen Ihre Kreditkarte vor und fragen nach einer Quittung.	Sie bejahen. Sie bitten den Gast zu unterschreiben.
Sie unterschreiben, bedanken sich und verabschieden sich.	Sie verabschieden sich und wünschen dem Gast eine gute Reise.

UNIT 12

3 Talking prices and numbers

a) Listen to the CD. Now it's your turn to read aloud.

1 That'll be €167.30 please.
2 There's a 12% reduction if you pay by 4th May.
3 Do you want to pay the mini-bar bill now? It's $12.50.
4 Your room number is 738. It's on the 7th floor.
5 Our bank account number is 45678890. The amount payable is €379.23 plus V.A.T.

b) Now you are listening to some hotel guests. Write down the five numbers you hear.

1 A time: _____
2 The right room number: _____
3 The wrong room number: _____
4 A telephone number: _____
5 The country code: _____

4 Questions

The guest does not understand some of the expressions on the bill.

A What does "Überweisen Sie" mean? _____
B What does "Mehrwertsteuer" mean? _____
C What does "Zahlen Sie innerhalb" mean? _____
D What does "in bar erhalten" mean? _____

Can you help? Here are some words and phrases to help you.

… is included in the bill.
It means you should/must …
cash payment(s)
bank account
transfer money
pay within … days
Only … will be accepted
use a credit card
Value Added Tax

27

UNIT 13

The world of food

1 Different types of food

Here are some different foods. Put them into the categories below. Then find a partner and compare your category lists. Are they the same?

> asparagus • chicken • turkey • tomatoes •
> milk • gherkins • potatoes • mushrooms •
> ham • lamb • aubergines • Brussel sprouts •
> cabbage • beef • onions • duck • venison •
> cod • beans • lettuce • garlic • boiled ham •
> liver pâté • carrots • pork • liver • cheese •
> pepper • cream • plaice • pears • eels

1 Vegetables: _____

2 Poultry: _____

3 Fruit: _____

4 Meat: _____

5 Game: _____

6 Spices: _____

7 Cold cuts: _____

8 Dairy products: _____

9 Fish: _____

2 That looks good!

Match these food specialities with the descriptions below.
1 Gulasch mit Knödel
2 Wienerschnitzel mit Pommes frites
3 Schweinshaxe mit Kartoffeln und Sauerkraut
4 Gebratener Schweinerücken mit einer dunklen Soße
5 Gebratene Tomaten gefüllt mit Schafskäse
6 Tafelspitz mit Salzkartoffeln
7 Kaiserschmarren
8 Powidlknödel (Hefeknödel mit Pflaumenmus) mit Vanillesoße

> A This is a thin slice of fried veal which is covered with breadcrumbs and served with French fries.
> B Ideal as a starter! Stuffed tomatoes fried with a goat's cheese filling.
> C Loin of fried pork which is served with a delicious red wine gravy.
> D Knuckle of pork with potatoes and a generous portion of pickled cabbage.
> E These are mouth-sized cubes of braised beef in a rich and spicy brown gravy, served with potato dumplings.
> F A delicious Austrian speciality: a warm yeast dumpling filled with plum jam and covered with custard.
> G A simple but tasty traditional dish: stewed beef filet with boiled potatoes.
> H A meal fit for an emperor: pancake strips with caramelised raisins.

1 ___ , 2 ___ , 3 ___ , 4 ___ , 5 ___ , 6 ___ , 7 ___ , 8 ___

UNIT 13

3 Describing food

a) Read this text on food and find the English words in the text which correspond to the German words underneath the text. You can either use a dictionary or work with a partner.

> If you work in a restaurant, the easiest way of helping guests when they choose food is to give them your menu in their own language. If you don't have one of these, there may be difficulties. Then you need to describe the dishes on the menu. Eggs, for example, can be fried, scrambled, poached or boiled. Meat can be fried, grilled, braised, boiled or even
> 5 roasted. Potatoes can be fried, boiled, mashed or sliced and fried in a fryer and served as chips – Americans call them French fries. Don't forget either, the three ways of serving steak: rare, medium or well done.
> A very useful expression to use when describing food is "It's a (special) kind of …" After this expression you can compare it with something your guest (or you) might know from
> 10 their country. "Königsberger Klopse," for example, could be described like this: "It's a kind of small to medium-sized meatball served in a creamy sauce with capers." Other useful expressions are: "It's a mixture of (this) and (that)" and "It's like …". If you are in real trouble, you can just say: "It's a regional speciality", but don't forget to add: "And it's delicious."

1 Gerichte _____
2 pochiert _____
3 gebraten _____
4 geschmort _____
5 sahnig _____
6 in Scheiben geschnitten _____
7 durch _____
8 köstlich _____

b) Work with a partner:
Describe your favourite dish in English. Can your partner guess what it is?

4 What did the waitress say?

Look at the guest's answers. What questions did the waitress ask?

1 Would _____?
   – No, thanks. I really couldn't manage an ice cream.

2 Would _____?
   – No thanks, I won't bother with a starter.

3 How _____ coffee? – Yes, good idea!

4 How _____? – Rare, please.

5 Would _____?
   – Yes, please! I've heard a lot about Austrian cakes.

UNIT 14

Food specialities

1 Different combinations

When we are talking about food certain words go together naturally. Match up the words on the left with those on the right.

1	Spare	A	chips
2	Sweet and sour	B	lamb
3	Leg of	C	and Yorkshire pudding
4	Steak	D	ribs
5	Turkey	E	pork
6	Lamb	F	and kidney pie
7	Roast beef	G	and stuffing
8	Fish and	H	chops

1 ___ , 2 ___ , 3 ___ , 4 ___ ,
5 ___ , 6 ___ , 7 ___ , 8 ___

2 The right word

Listen to the CD and then translate the German words and complete the text.

> carve • consists • flavour • light •
> medium-bodied • sharp • stuffing • thyme

WAITER: Have you made up your mind, sir? I can definitely recommend the wild turkey with (**1.** *Füllung*) _____

MR BAXTER: Yes, I think I'll have that, please.
But tell me, what's the difference between normal turkey and wild turkey?

WAITER: Well, simply, wild turkey has more (**2.** *Geschmack*) _____ .
MR BAXTER: Oh good!

WAITER: Shall I (**3.** *zerlegen*) _____ it at the table?

MR BAXTER: No, that won't be necessary, thank you. Can you tell me what the stuffing is?

WAITER: Yes. It mainly (**4.** *besteht*) _____ of parsley and (**5.** *Thymian*) _____ .

MR BAXTER: Sounds delicious! And what would you like, darling?
MRS BAXTER: I think I'll go for the rack of lamb.
WAITER: Right, fine. And I'll make sure you get a (**6.** *scharfes*) _____ steak knife, madam.
MRS BAXTER: Thank you.
MR BAXTER: And what kind of wine would you recommend?

WAITER: I would suggest a (**7.** *mittelkräftigen*) _____ red wine with the lamb and a (**8.** *leichten*) _____ white wine with the turkey.

 Now listen to the CD again and check your answers.

UNIT 14

3 Preparing steaks

Listen to the talk and do the exercises that follow. You may listen to the talk as often as you like.

> Georg Gustl is training a younger colleague in his kitchen to become a chef. The trainee, Michael, can't yet speak much German so Georg is explaining to him in English how to trim, cut and cook steaks.

a) Imagine you want to give a similar talk a few weeks later. Make brief notes, using the following headings:

Cutting the steak: 1 _____
2 _____
3 _____

Producing cuts for: 1 Tournedos? _____
2 Fillet steaks? _____

The steak is tough? Answer to problem: _____
_____

b) Can you pronounce the following words correctly?
Listen to the CD and check them again.

> angle • knives • fibres • tough • edge • sinew • thickest • section • slicing

4 What's that speciality?

Read the following descriptions of German and Austrian specialities and choose which one you think it is. Write your answers under the descriptions.

> Apfelstrudel • Kaiserschmarren • Leberknödel • Maultaschen • Weißwurst

1 This is a kind of pasta. It looks a little like Italian ravioli but does not always have a meat filling, sometimes it is spinach.

_____

2 This is eaten as a dessert and is well-known in Austria. It's a very sweet, rich pancake that is pulled apart in the frying pan and often served with caramelised raisins and stewed plums.

_____

3 This consists of pieces of baked apple served in puff pastry and it is usually served with ice cream or whipped cream.

_____

4 They are basically meatballs; the meat is liver and they are often served in a clear beef broth.

_____

5 This is a special white sausage which is popular in Bavaria and it is eaten with sweet mustard and pretzels and preferably before midday.

_____

UNIT 15

The tools of the kitchen and restaurant

1 Pots and pans and kitchen tools

Look at the kitchen utensils below and label them with words from the box.

> 2 chopping block • casserole dish 10
> 6 food processor • frying pan • grater 8 ✓
> 7 scales • serrated knife • sieve 4
> 9 two-pronged fork • whisk 3

5 _____
9 _____
6 _____
7 _____
3 _____
8 Raspel
4 _____
1 _____
2 _____
10 _____

2 Spoons and spatulas (wenden)

a) Name these things with the words from the box.
Write the words next to the photos.

> 2 fish slice • 4 gravy spoon • ladle 3
> 5 spatula • wooden spoon 1

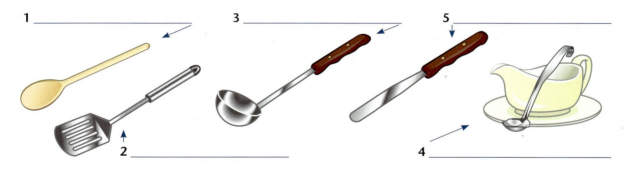

1 _____
3 _____
5 _____
2 _____
4 _____

b) Match the descriptions below with the pictures above.

A The thin wide blade is ideal for lifting delicate portions of fish from a baking tray. Fish slice
B The thin narrow blade is useful for spreading and smoothing things such as cake mixes. Spatula
C This is used to serve portions of gravy or sauce. gravy spoon
D It's often used for stirring soups and sauces. Wooden spoon
E This is like a very big, deep spoon and it's used to serve portions of soup. Ladle

1 D
2 A
3 E
4 C
5 B

c) Work with a partner:
Think of an elaborate dish and make a list in English of all the kitchen tools and equipment you would need to make it.

3 Where do we put the food?

a) Here is a list of food and drink. Below the list are the names of different types of containers. With a partner decide where the food and drink could be kept or stored.

butter • grapes • bread • cashew nuts • gravy • margarine • maple syrup • apples • bananas • coffee • tea • jam • honey • sugar • milk • strawberries • pineapples • yogurt • bread rolls • croissants

1 A bowl of	2 A jug of	3 A pot of	4 A dish of	5 A basket of
grapes	gravy	coffee	butter	rolls

b) Work with a partner: Write and act dialogues between guests and a waiter or waitress.
For Example:
Excuse me, I can't find the yogurt. – It's in the tall jug next to the ...

4 Setting the table

a) Identify the objects on the table.

salt and pepper set • water glass • coffee spoon • plate • knife • dessert fork • wine glass • vase • fork • serviette • coffee cup • soup spoon • sugar bowl • bread basket • dessert spoon • saucer

1 _____
2 _____
3 _____
4 _____
5 _____
6 _____
7 _____
8 _____
9 _____
10 _____
11 _____
12 _____
13 _____
14 _____
15 _____
16 _____

b) Work with a partner: Imagine that you have to explain to a trainee how to set a table.
Where does the ... go? – It goes next to/above/below the ...

UNIT 16

The chef

1 Local produce and quality ingredients

> A Schnittlauch • B hinzufügen •
> C Topfen/Quark • D schmackhaft •
> E Lieferanten • F Kümmel •
> G gebraut • H hiesig •
> I Rezept • J im Grunde •
> K gewürzt • L Wacholderbeere

a) Read the following interview with the head chef of a top quality restaurant in the Tyrol. Match the words in red with the German words in the box.

INTERVIEWER:	Today we're talking to Herr Bergmann about the ingredients he needs for the specialities on offer in his restaurant. Herr Bergmann, where do you buy your produce?
HERR BERGMANN:	I always try and buy food which is locally grown. I think my guests like the idea that the food on their plate comes from this area because they are then sure that it is fresh. It's also good for the local economy. I know my **suppliers (1)** well and can ask them where the food comes from and I know they give me an honest answer.
INTERVIEWER:	What sort of produce do you look for?
HERR BERGMANN:	Well, we're only a small hotel with a small restaurant. We only have a few dishes on our menu but we want the best possible produce for those dishes. All of our specialities are unique to our restaurant.
INTERVIEWER:	And what are these special dishes?
HERR BERGMANN:	Well, we do a beer soup and a garlic soup and we insist on using **local (2)** light beer for the beer soup. This beer is an importat ingredient in several of our dishes. We also do a traditional Austrian Coachman's salad. For that our local supplier produces an Italian-style Bologna sausage which is very **tasty (3)** and comes from a secret **recipe (4)**. One of our most popular meat dishes is "Innviertler Surbradl".
INTERVIEWER:	What on earth is that?
HERR BERGMANN:	Well, it's **basically (5)** braised pork but its special flavour comes from the locally grown **juniper berries (6)** and locally **brewed (7)** beer which we **add (8)**. Another speciality is our beer cheese spread which is made from "Quargel".
INTERVIEWER:	"Quargel"? That sounds interesting. What is that?
HERR BERGMANN:	"Quargel" is a soft, sour-milk cheese. This is mixed with **curd cheese (9)**, chopped onion and **chives (10)** and beer. This is then **seasoned (11)** with red pepper salt and **caraway (12)**.
INTERVIEWER:	That sounds tasty. Do you have any other specialities?
HERR BERGMANN:	Well, we also do our own beer rolls, which go well with the cheese spread.

1 ___ , 2 ___ , 3 ___ , 4 ___ , 5 ___ , 6 ___ , 7 ___ , 8 ___ , 9 ___ , 10 ___ , 11 ___ , 12 ___

b) If you were a waiter or waitress in Mr Bergmann's restaurant which two selling points would you mention to the guests?

1. _____   2. _____

_____   _____

_____   _____

UNIT 16

2 Tips from the boss

Your new boss Dan Thomas has given his staff some tips on how to prepare vegetables. He doesn't speak German. Use the words in the box to complete the following text.

> amount • buttered • densely • garnishing • matures • peeling • raw • skin • squeeze • soggy

Spinach:
This is delicious (1) _____ with a (2) _____ of lemon and garlic.

Cabbage:
Most cabbages are best cooked for 5–7 minutes in a minimal (3) _____ of water.

Watercress:
It may be cooked in soups, pies and pancakes, or eaten (4) _____ in salads.

Mustard and cress:
This is excellent for (5) _____ or mixing into rice dishes.

Broccoli:
Remember to buy this during the right season! It (6) _____ in winter rather than summer or autumn.

White or Dutch cabbage:
This is (7) _____ packed and excellent for salads.

General notes:
All vegetables, whether to be served cooked or raw, should be washed quickly under a stream of cold water. The only exception to this are mushrooms, which can become (8) _____ and should therefore only be wiped carefully with a clean dry cloth.

(9) _____ root vegetables should be avoided as a large portion of the vitamin content is found just beneath the (10) _____

Happy cooking!

Dan

3 Helping the boss

Dan comes to you with _____. Can you help him?
Match the German _____.

1 leicht verde_____   _____ date
2 Haltbark_____   _____l, dry place
3 Nicht wiec_____
4 Enthält keine_____
5 Eier aus Freiland_____
6 Ofen vorheizen_____
7 Kühl und trocken aufbe_____   _____ additives

1 ___, 2 ___, 3 ___, 4 ___, 5 ___, _____

UNIT 17

Fish and shellfish

1 Fish or shellfish?

Are these food items freshwater fish, saltwater fish or shellfish?
Put them in the correct list.

cockles • perch • cod • crab • herring • trout • haddock • lobster • salmon • sole • carp • mussels • plaice • rainbow trout • brown trout • prawns

Freshwater fish:
_____
_____
_____
_____
_____
_____

Saltwater fish:
_____
_____
_____
_____
_____
_____

Shellfish:
_____
_____
_____
_____
_____
_____

2 How is it cooked?

a) Guests may ask you how the fish is prepared or cooked. There are at least half a dozen ways. Do you know them? Listen to the following dialogues and complete the sentences with these words.

baked • batter • breadcrumbs • deep fry • grilled • marinate • poached • steam

1 Their trout is _____.

2 Their sole is _____ and stuffed with prawns.

3 Their cod is usually fried in _____.

   But it can also be fried in _____.

4 The woman prefers the salmon _____

5 They _____ the cod.

6 They _____ the salmon.

7 They _____ the fish first.

UNIT 17

3 Delicious fish recipes

a) Apart from the fish dishes already mentioned there are a number of more exotic fish dishes a restaurant might offer, including fish we don't see very often on menus. Look at the following descriptions of fish dishes in German and match them with the recipes in English.

1
Kleine Stücke von Flussbarsch auf einem Spieß, garniert mit Zwiebeln, Tomaten, Lorbeerblättern und kleinen Zitronestückchen.

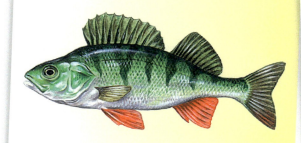

2
Marinierter Seebarsch gebacken mit schwarzen Oliven, Tomaten, Koriander, und eine Scheibe Zitrone in einer Keramikform.

A
Combine chopped coriander with crushed garlic, 2 tablespoons of olive oil, 1 tablespoon of cumin, 2 tablespoons of paprika, salt, hot red peppers and half a glass of water. Gut, scale and rinse the bass and cut into pieces. Mix the above with 6 tablespoons of olive oil, saffron and ginger and marinate the fish in this for 2 hours. Roast peppers in the oven, put them in a greased oven dish. Put the fish on top of the peppers along with two ripe tomatoes and the rest of the marinade and bake for 45 minutes at 160 degrees Celsius. Then serve with black olives.

B
Combine 12 tablespoons of olive oil and the juice of 1 lemon in a bowl, add a pinch of salt and pepper and 1 tablespoon of cumin. Gut, wash, skin and filet the perch; cut it into bite size pieces and marinate in the oil and lemon for 30 minutes. Prepare the skewers, alternating a piece of fish, tomato slice, bay leaf, lemon slice and onion. Cook over a charcoal grill for about 20 minutes, baste often with the marinade. Serve hot with parsley, bay leaves and lemon slices.

1 ___ , 2 ___

b) How would you translate these words into German?

1 chopper (n.) _____   chop (v.) _____
2 crush (v.) _____   crushed (adj.) _____
3 gut (n.) _____   gutted (adj.) _____
4 scale (n.) _____   descaled (adj.) _____
5 grease (n.) _____   grease (v.) _____
6 skin (n.) _____   skinned (adj.) _____

UNIT 18

Are you a vegetarian?

1 Interview with a chef

Listen to this interview.
Now listen again and answer
the following questions
by circling the correct letter.

1 The interviewer
   is a journalist from …
   a a local newspaper.
   b a magazine.
   c a radio programme.

2 Mr Groetzel works
   at the "Wiener
   Burgklausel" as a …
   a waiter.
   b chef.
   c manager.

3 The topic of the
   interview is …
   a vegetarian cooking.
   b party catering.
   c confectionary.

4 A vegan is
   someone who …
   a loves vegetables.
   b shares a flat.
   c doesn't eat any
      animal products.

5 Mr Groetzel is very proud of his
   speciality: his strudel is filled with …
   a minced chicken.
   b bacon and spinach.
   c sauerkraut.

2 Opposites and synonyms

a) Listen to the interview again and find the opposites of these words:

1 unhealthy _____   4 unpopular _____
2 high _____   5 unimaginative _____
3 easy _____   6 boring _____

b) Find three synonyms for the word "tasty".

1. d_____   2. m_____   3. s_____

3 Who are they?

Here are three regular guests at Mr Groetzel's restaurant.
Look at the information in the box.
Look at what they say. Write their names under the photos.

Mrs Giddens is a vegan.
Mr Stanley is a vegetarian.
Mr Salideh is a Muslim.

I eat some meat,
mutton and chicken mostly.
I don't eat any pork.

I don't eat meat
or fish, but lots of
yoghurt and eggs.

I don't eat any
animal products
at all.

1. _____   2. _____   3. _____

4 Healthy diet tips

diet • high-fibre • delicious • red meat • fat content • fresh • sugary • low-fat • vitamins

Use these words to fill in the gaps:

1 Don't eat _____ desserts, eat _____ fruit.
2 There are lots of _____ products on the market today.
3 Eat more vegetables, they contain a lot of _____.
4 Beans and nuts are _____ foods.
5 This recipe book contains many _____ dishes.
6 Fruit and vegetables are part of a balanced _____.
7 If you want to lose weight, you've got to reduce the _____ of your meals.
8 Reduce the amount of _____ and eat more fish and chicken.

5 Special needs

Work with a partner and plan a vegetarian menu for one day. Write the names of all the dishes in English, of course!

Breakfast: _____

Lunch: _____

Dinner: _____

UNIT 19

Having a drink

1 Getting the drinks

Look at the phrases 1–5 below. They are all answers to questions asked by guests when ordering drinks. Then look at the questions A–E and match them with the correct answer.

1 No, it's really quite a dark beer, in fact.
2 Well, it's cultivated in the Burgundy region of France.
3 That's very kind of you, but I'm not allowed to drink when on duty.
4 Not really, it's more like your lager, except without the chemicals.
5 Well, I wouldn't really recommend that wine with that meat.

A I'm thinking of choosing the Riesling with the braised beef. What do you think?
B Is it a light beer?
C Where does the wine come from?
D Can I buy you a drink? You've given us excellent service.
E Is that beer like our bitter beer back home?

A ___
B ___
C ___
D ___
E ___

2 Describing the drinks

Complete the descriptions below and decide which German or Austrian drinks the staff are describing to guests.

thin • diluting • frothy • equivalent • digestive

Sekt • Obstbrand/Obstler • Kölsch • Gespritzter/Weinschorle • Weizenbier

1 _____ must be poured very carefully and slowly out of the bottle as it is very _____ . It's often even served with a slice of lemon.

2 _____ is the German _____ of French champagne, but of course it isn't quite as expensive. In Britain it's often called champagne even when it hasn't actually come from the champagne region of France.

3 _____ is a special beer from Cologne. It is light and fresh and is served in small, _____ glasses.

4 Fruit schnapps is called _____ .
   In Austria people often drink it after a meal as a _____ .

5 A "_____" is a way of _____ the alcohol. You simply mix wine with sparkling water.

UNIT 19

3 Exotic drinks

bar spoon • straws • shaker • ice tongs • blender • strainer • mixing glass • ice scoop • dash bottle

Beer and wine are the traditional drinks people often associate with meals. But as you know, not everyone drinks wine or beer. Teetotallers only drink soft drinks, such as orange juice or mineral water, and no alcohol. Some guests have more exotic tastes and want to try out the latest cocktails, with or without alcohol. To prepare and serve these drinks, special tools and equipment are needed.

a) Look at the pictures below and name each item using these words.

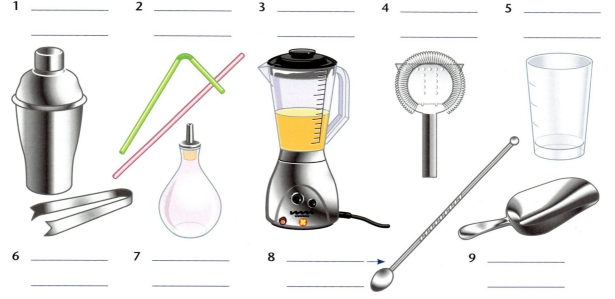

1 _____   2 _____   3 _____   4 _____   5 _____

6 _____   7 _____   8 _____   9 _____

b) Work with a partner. What are these things called in German?

4 Small talk at the bar

Work with a partner and practise some small talk. Use the phrases below to help you get started.

For some people, "small talk" doesn't come easily. However, it is often important when dealing with British or American guests. Here's a useful tip: Listen to what the guest says and make a sympathetic reply. This shows that you're listening. You can then add something that shows sympathy or ask a question which invites the guest to say more.

A guest:
- I've had such a terrible day.
- I've had a really great day!
- Is the weather always this bad here?
- It's my birthday today!
- I don't feel very well today.
- I've just been told that I've got a new job!
- …

You:
- Have you? That's good/terrible/…
- Is it? Happy Birthday!
  I'll get you a drink on the house.
- Bad? It's usually much worse.
- Oh I'm sorry to hear that. Can I help at all?
- Congratulations! That's great news.
  When do you start?
- …

UNIT 20

Commercial catering

1 Starting a new job with a commercial caterer

Frank Jenkins has just started a new job with "Hot food services" and his boss, Melanie Beaver, is explaining the job to him.
The sentences below describe words in the text. What are they?

Melanie: Welcome on board, Frank! Are you looking forward to your first day? You'll meet 18 of our best customers.
Frank: Yes, but I have a couple of questions. Do I drive to the same clients every day?
Melanie: Normally yes, but you will get different routes after two or three months.
Frank: I'm carrying 15 tons of food. Is it all pre-packed?
Melanie: Again, normally yes, but sometimes you will have to do special runs with fresh food. Just a couple of other things, Frank. We are marketing a new range of hot cupboards and ice machines and we want you to take the new brochures with you today. And when you visit private companies, don't forget to inform the event manager that we can provide casual catering assistants whenever they need them. This is a new service.
Frank: No problem.

1 Equipment which keeps food warm for a long period of time: _____

2 People who work part time and only when they are needed: _____

3 Another word for customer: _____

4 Somebody who organises social events for their company: _____

5 Another word for deliveries: _____

6 Food which is stored in special boxes to keep fresh: _____

T14 2 Frank on tour

Frank's conversation with a customer has been mixed up. Put it in the right order and then check your result with the dialogue on the CD

A **Frank:** Yes, of course. I'll put your order through right now.
B **Customer:** Fine, I'll do that.
C **Frank:** Sorry, that's not really my job. Is it one of our machines?
D **Customer:** Thanks very much. There's just one more thing: we're having some trouble with our ice machine at the moment. Could you help?
E **Frank:** Good morning. You ordered 200 pies, 25 bags of cocktail tomatoes and 50 loaves?
F **Customer:** Yes, bye!
G **Frank:** See you tomorrow then.
H **Customer:** Yes that's right. Thanks. Could we have the same again tomorrow?
I **Frank:** I'll give you our technician's business card. If you ring him now, he could come out and see you today.
J **Customer:** Yes, here's the guarantee.

___ ___ ___ ___ ___ ___ ___ ___ ___ ___

UNIT **20**

3 Fitting out the bar

You have written to Bar World Specialists GmbH to enquire about setting up a new bar. They have sent you information about their products and services. Fill in the gaps using the words below.

dispensing • clothing • mats • interior • register • equipment

To help you make your new bar a great success, we can provide

1 cash _____ ,
2 beer _____ ,
3 professional _____ for bar staff,
4 _____ for making ice cubes and crushed ice,
5 _____ and exterior bar design,
6 drink _____ equipment.

4 Advertising your catering services

Your boss wants to write an advertising brochure for your hotel's catering services but she doesn't know certain words. Can you help her?

Organising an office party soon? A company party? A conference? Or does your company have a **Fest** (1) _____ coming up? Do you need top quality finger food, buffet arrangements, a sit-down meal or banquet?

THEN GET IN TOUCH WITH US SOON! BIG EVENTS ARE OUR SPECIALITY!

We **liefern** (2) _____ all types of food for all tastes and

Anlässe (3) _____ .

provide **gratis** (4) _____ champagne for events costing more than € 2.000,

provide **Zelte** (5) _____ for open-air

Veranstaltungen (6) _____ ,

provide all necessary **Geschirr** (7) _____

and **Besteck** (8) _____ .

HOTEL WINGATE • DODDERINGTON
BERKS BN13 6PQ • TEL. (0044) 1740 656 831   **WINGATE**Hotel

43

Technical wordlist

A
across – *(Rätsel) waagerecht*
access – *Zugang*
accommodation – *Unterkunft*
account number – *Kontonummer*
add – *hinzufügen*
additional – *zusätzlich*
advance: in ~ *im Voraus*
air conditioning – *Klimaanlage*
anticipated – *voraussichtlich*
apology – *Entschuldigung*
apparatus – *Gerät, Ausrüstung*
application form – *Antragsformular*
appropriate – *geeignet, passend*
artificial additive – *künstlicher Zusatzstoff*
ashtray – *Aschenbecher*
asparagus – *Spargel*
availability – *Verfügbarkeit*

B
bake – *backen*
baked – *gebacken*
bank account – *Bankkonto*
bar of soap – *ein Stück Seife*
barley – *Gerste*
bar spoon – *Messlöffel*
basket – *Korb*
bass – *Barsch*
bay leaf – *Lorbeerblatt*
beer mat – *Bierdeckel*
bill – *Rechnung; (nur AE) Geldschein*
blender – *Mixer*
blunt – *stumpf*
boil – *kochen, sieden*
booking – *Buchung, Bestellung*
bone (a fish) – *entgräten*
bottle opener – *Flaschenöffner*
bowl – *Schüssel, Schale*
bracket – *Klammer*
breadcrumbs – *Paniermehl*
bread roll – *Brötchen*
braise – *schmoren*
braised – *geschmort*
braised beef – *Tafelspitz*
braised steak – *Schmorfleisch*
brandy – *Weinbrand*
brewed – *gebraut*
broth – *Brühe*
brown trout – *Bachforelle*
Brussel sprouts – *Rosenkohl, Kohlsprossen*

C
cabbage – *Kohl*
cancel – *(Event:) absagen, streichen; (Bestellung:) stornieren, abbestellen*
caper – *Kaper*
caraway – *Kümmel*
carp – *Karpfen*
case (suitcase) – *Koffer*
cash register – *Kasse*
casserole dish – *Bräter, Schmortopf, Auflaufform*
caterer – *Lieferant(in) von Speisen und Getränken*
catering – *Partyservice, Catering*
chambermaid – *Zimmermädchen*
charge – *berechnen*
check in – *sich im Hotel anmelden; Anmeldung*
cherry – *Kirsche*
chicken – *Hähnchen*
chive(s) – *Schnittlauch*
chop – *hacken, klein schneiden; Kotelett*
chopping block – *Hackbrett, (Hackstock)*
chunk – *großes Stück*
cider – *(BE:) Apfelwein, Cidre; (AE:) Apfelsaft*
circle – *Kreis; einen Kringel um etwas machen*
click on – *(Computer:) etwas anklicken*
client – *Klient(in)*
clothing – *Kleidung*
coat hanger – *Kleiderbügel*
cockle – *Herzmuschel*
cod – *Kabeljau*
cold cuts – *(Wurst) Aufschnitt*
colleague – *Kollege, Kollegin*
column – *(bei einer Tabelle) Spalte*
complaint – *Beschwerde*
complete – *vollständig; vervollständigen*
complimentary drink – *freies Getränk, Getränk auf's Haus*
concerning – *betreffend*
condensed milk – *Kondensmilch*
confirm – *bestätigen*
confirmation – *Bestätigung*
consist of … – *bestehen aus …*
control panel – *Bedienungskonsole*
conversation – *Unterhaltung, Gespräch*
corked – *(Wein:) verkorkt*
corkscrew – *Korkenzieher*
country code – *(Telefon) Landesvorwahl*
cover – *Deckel; zudecken*
crab – *Taschenkrebs*
crispy – *knusprig*
crockery – *Geschirr*
crush – *zermalmen*
cube – *Würfel*
cumin – *Kreuzkümmel*
curd cheese – *Quark, Topfen*
currency – *Währung*
curtains – *Gardinen, Vorhänge*
customer – *Kunde, Kundin*
cutlery – *Besteck*

D
dairy – *Molkerei*
dairy products – *Milch-/Molkereiprodukte*
Danish pastry – *Plundergebäck*
dash bottle – *Spritzflasche*
deadline – *letzter Termin*
deep fry – *frittieren*
delicious – *köstlich*
delivery – *Lieferung*
departure – *Abreise*
dessert – *Nachtisch, Nachspeise, Dessert*
digestive – *Verdauungs-*

Technical wordlist

diluted – *verdünnt*
direction – *Richtung*
directions – *Wegbeschreibung; Anleitung*
disabled – *behindert*
disabled access – *für Behinderte zugänglich*
disabled persons – *Behinderte*
dish – *Schüssel, Schale; Gericht, Speise*
dishes – *Geschirr*
dispensing (drinks) – *(Getränke) austeilen*
drink dispensing equipment – *Zapfanlage*
duck – *Ente*
dumpling – *Knödel, Kloß*
double room – *Doppelzimmer*
down – *(Rätsel) senkrecht*
duties – *Aufgaben*
duty – *Pflicht; Dienst*

E
ensure – *gewährleisten*
equipment – *Ausrüstung; Ausstattung*
equivalent – *entsprechend; Entsprechung, Pendant*
evaporated milk – *Kondensmilch*
event – *Veranstaltung*
excursion – *Ausflug*
exhibitor – *Aussteller(in)*
explanation – *Erklärung*
expression – *Ausdruck*

F
facilities – *Einrichtungen, Anlagen*
filling – *Füllung*
finalize – *festlegen, beschließen*
fit: What doesn't …? – *Was passt nicht?*
flan – *Obsttorte*
flour – *Mehl*
food processor – *Küchenmaschine*
fork – *Gabel*
free-range eggs – *Eier aus Freilandhaltung*
French fries – *Pommes frites*
freshwater fish – *Süßwasserfisch(e)*
fridge – *Kühlschrank*
fried egg – *Spiegelei*
frothy – *schaumig, mit Schaum*
fry – *in der Pfanne braten; frittieren*
fryer – *Fritteuse*
frying pan – *Bratpfanne*

G
game – *(Fleisch) Wild*
gap – *Lücke*
garlic – *Knoblauch*
garnishing – *Garnierung*
generous – *großzügig*
a generous helping/portion – *eine große Portion*
gherkin – *Essiggurke*
ghost – *Gespenst*
ginger – *Ingwer*
go well with sth. – *gut zu etwas passen*
goat's cheese – *Ziegenkäse*
grape – *Weintraube*
grater – *Reibe, Raspel, Reibeisen*

gravy – *Bratensoße*
grease – *Fett; einfetten*
greetings – *Grüße*
guest – *Gast*
gut – *ausnehmen, ausweiden*
guts – *Eingeweide*

H
habit – *Gewohnheit*
haddock – *Schellfisch*
ham – *Schinken*
handle – *Klinke, Knauf; Griff, Henkel; Bügel, Stiel*
head chef – *Küchenchef(in)*
helping – *(Mahlzeit) Portion*
second helping – *Nachschlag*
herbs – *Gewürze, Kräuter*
honeymoon – *Flitterwochen*
hot cupboard – *Wärmeschrank*
hotel register – *Gästebuch*
housekeeper – *Haushälter(in)*

I
ice cube – *Eiswürfel*
ice scoop – *Eisschaufel*
ice tongs – *Eiszange*
… is included – *… ist inbegriffen, inklusive*
ingredients – *Zutaten*

J
jam – *Marmelade*
journey – *Reise*
jug – *Krug*
juniper berry – *Wacholderbeere*

K
keen on – *sehr gern mögen*
key – *Schlüssel; Lösungsschlüssel*
kipper – *Räucherhering, Bückling*
knuckle of pork – *Eisbein*

L
ladle – *Suppenkelle, Schöpflöffel*
laundry – *Wäsche*
laundry service – *Wäscheservice*
lay the table – *Tisch decken*
leader – *Führer(in)*
leg of lamb – *Lammkeule*
lettuce – *Salatkopf, grüner Salat*
lobster – *Hummer*
loin – *(Fleisch) Lendenstück*
luggage – *Gepäck*
lunchtime specials – *Mittagskarte*

M
main course – *(Essen) Hauptgang*
mash – *Püree; etwas pürieren, stampfen*
mashed potato(es) – *Kartoffelpüree*
mat (beer) – *Bierdeckel*
match – *zusammenpassen; übereinstimmen*
mature – *reif; (heran)reifen*
meat – *Fleisch*

Technical wordlist

meatball – *Fleischklops, Fleischbällchen*
meats – *versch. Fleischarten*
medium (rare) – *(Steak) halb durchgebraten*
midnight – *Mitternacht*
mince – *Hackfleisch, Faschiertes; Fleisch durchdrehen bzw. klein hacken, faschieren*
mirror – *Spiegel*
mixing glass – *Rührschüssel*
mixture – *Mischung*
mobile – *beweglich, mobil*
mobile phone – *Handy*
mushroom soup – *Pilzsuppe*
mussel – *Miesmuschel*
mustard – *Senf*

N
nappy (AE: diaper) – *Windel*
non-smoker – *Nichtraucher(in)*
notepad – *Notizblock*
notice – *Bekanntmachung, Anschlag; etwas zur Kenntnis nehmen*

O
odd one out: Which is the …? – *Welches gehört nicht dazu?/Was passt nicht?*
onion – *Zwiebel*
order – *Bestellung; bestellen*
overnight – *über Nacht*
overnight accommodation – *Übernachtung*

P
pancake – *Pfannkuchen, Palatschinken*
parking space – *einzelner Parkplatz*
parsley – *Petersilie*
participant – *Teilnehmer(in)*
pastry – *Teig*
pastries – *Gebäck*
pastry chef – *Konditor(in)*
payment – *Bezahlung*
pear – *Birne*
peel – *Schale; schälen*
peelings – *Schalen*
perch – *Flussbarsch*
perishable – *leicht verderblich*
pickles – *eingelegtes Gemüse*
pie – *Teigtasche, z. B. Fleischpastete, gedeckter Obstkuchen*
pig – *Schwein*
pillow – *Kopfkissen, Kopfpolster*
pinch: a … of – *eine Prise*
pineapple – *Ananas*
plaice – *Scholle*
plum – *Pflaume, Zwetschke*
poached egg – *pochiertes Ei*
polite – *höflich*
porter – *(am Bahnhof oder Flughafen:) Gepäckträger(in); (im Hotel:) Pförtner(in), Portier, Portiersfrau*
postpone – *verschieben, aufschieben*
pot – *Topf*
poultry – *Geflügel*

prawn – *Garnele*
prefer sth. to sth. – *etwas vorziehen, bevorzugen*
pre-heat – *vorheizen*
prepare – *(Mahlzeit) zubereiten*
process – *Vorgang*
provided (that) – *vorausgesetzt, (dass) …*
provided (with) – *vorgegeben; zur Verfügung gestellt*
puff pastry – *Blätterteig*

Q
quoted – *(Preise:) genannt, zitiert*

R
radish – *Radieschen*
rainbow trout – *Regenbogenforelle*
raisin – *Rosine*
rare – *(Steak) englisch, 'blutig'*
raspberry – *Himbeere*
raw – *roh, ungekocht*
ready for a holiday – *urlaubsreif*
reception – *Hotelempfang*
receipt – *Beleg, Quittung*
receptionist – *Empfangschef, Empfangsdame*
recipe – *(Koch-)Rezept*
recommend sth. to sb. – *jemandem etwas empfehlen*
reduct ion – *Reduzierung; Preisnachlass, Ermäßigung*
(With my/best/kindest) regards – *(Briefschluss:) Mit freundlichen Grüßen*
refreshments – *Erfrischungen; Getränke*
registration form – *Anmeldeformular*
request – *Bitte; um etwas bitten*
require – *brauchen, benötigen*
remote control – *Fernbedienung*
renew – *(Buchung:) wiederholen, verlängern*
replenish – *(wieder) auffüllen*
reply – *Antwort; antworten, erwidern*
reservation – *Reservierung, Buchung*
reserve – *reservieren, buchen*
responsible – *verantwortlich*
not responsible for … – *nicht haftbar für …*
revolting – *ekelhaft, widerlich*
rich – *(Essen) reichhaltig, schwer*
rinse – *(ab)spülen*
roast pork – *Schweinebraten*
(bread) roll – *Brötchen*

S
salmon – *Lachs*
salty – *salzig, gesalzen*
saltwater fish – *Meeresfisch(e)*
saucer – *Untertasse*
sausage – *Wurst*
sauté(d) – *kurz an(ge)braten*
sauté potatoes – *Bratkartoffeln*
savoury – *herzhaft, pikant*
scale – *Fischschuppen; Fisch (ab)schuppen*
scales – *Waage*
scrambled egg – *Rührei, Eierspeise*
screen – *TV Bildschirm, Computermonitor*
scrumptious – *lecker*
seasoned – *gewürzt*

select(ed) – *auswählen; (auserlesen)*
sell-by date – *Haltbarkeitsdatum*
serrated knife – *Sägemesser, Wellschliffmesser*
serve – *servieren; bedienen*
set the table – *Tisch decken*
shaker – *Mixbecher*
shellfish – *Schalentier(e)*
shower hose – *Duschschlauch*
sieve – *Sieb*
sign – *Zeichen, Schild; unterschreiben*
similar (to) – *ähnlich*
sinew – *Sehne*
single room – *Einzelzimmer*
skewer – *Spieß*
skillet – *Bratpfanne aus Gusseisen*
skimmer – *Schaumlöffel*
skin – *Haut; enthäuten*
slice: a … of – *Scheibe/Stück*
smoker – *Raucher(in)*
soggy – *durchweicht*
sold out – *ausverkauft*
sole – *Seezunge*
soup spoon – *Suppenlöffel*
sous chef – *Stellvertreter(in) des Küchenchefs*
sparkling wine – *Schaumwein*
spatula – *Bratenwender*
spice – *Gewürz*
spicy – *würzig, pikant*
spinach – *Spinat*
sprig of parsley – *Petersilienzweig*
spring onion – *Frühlingszwiebel*
squiggle – *Schnörkel*
staff – *Personal, Belegschaft*
starter – *Vorspeise*
steak knife – *Steakmesser, Fleischmesser*
steam – *Dampf; dämpfen*
stew – *schmoren; Eintopf*
stewed plums – *Pflaumenkompott, Zwetschkenkompott*
stir-fry – *unter Rühren kurz anbraten*
stock – *Waren; Waren vorrätig haben*
strainer – *Barsieb*
straw – *Trinkhalm*
strawberry – *Erdbeer*
stuff – *stopfen*
stuffing – *Füllung*
suitable – *passend, geeignet*
suitcase (case) – *Koffer*
suite (of rooms) – *Suite*
supplier – *Lieferant(in)*
supplies – *Vorräte*
supply – *Versorgung, Lieferung; versorgen, beliefern*
supply (and demand) – *Angebot (und Nachfrage)*
surname – *Familienname, Nachname*
switch – *Schalter*
sympathy – *Mitgefühl, Verständnis*

T

tablecloth – *Tischtuch*
tablespoon – *Esslöffel*
take-away – *Essen zum Mitnehmen*
tart – *Obsttörtchen*

taste – *Geschmack; schmecken*
tasty – *schmackhaft, lecker*
teetotaller – *Abstinenzler(in)*
tick – *Häkchen (✔); abhaken*
five times six – *fünf mal sechs*
toilet roll – *Toilettenpapier*
tough – *(Fleisch) zäh*
towel – *Handtuch, Badetuch*
transfer – *(Geld) Überweisung; (Daten) Übertragung*
trout – *Forelle*
turkey – *Truthahn, Pute(r)*
two-pronged fork – *zweizinkige Gabel*
twin room – *Zweibettzimmer*
twins – *Zwillinge*

U

unsavoury – *(Essen) fade*
unscramble – *entwirren, entschlüsseln*

V

value added tax (VAT) – *Mehrwertsteuer*
veal – *Kalbfleisch*
vegetable – *Gemüse*
vegetarian – *Vegetarier(in)*
venison – *Rehfleisch, Hirschfleisch*
view – *Aussicht; betrachten*
vinegar – *Essig*
voyage – *Seereise, Törn*

W

waiter – *Kellner(in)*
waiter service – *Bedienung*
wake-up call – *Weckruf*
wastepaper bin – *Papierkorb*
well-done – *(Steak) gut durchgebraten*
whipped cream – *Schlagsahne, Schlagobers*
whisk – *Schneebesen*
wholemeal – *Vollkorn-*

Y

yeast – *Hefe, Germ*

Z

zander – *Zander*

CONVERSION TABLES

Length:

1 inch = 2.54 cm
1 foot = 30.48 cm
1 yard = 91.44 cm
1 mile = 1.609 km

1 cm = 0.3937 inch
1 m   = 39.37 inch
1 km = 0.62137 mile

Area:

1 square inch (in^2) = 6.45 cm^2
1 square foot (ft^2) = 0.093 m^2
1 square mile (m^2)   = 2.59 km^2

1 cm^2 = 0.155 square inches
1 m^2 = 10.764 square feet
1 km^2 = 0.3861 square miles

Volume:

1 cubic inch (in^3) = 16.387 cm^3

1 pint (pt.)   = 0.57 l
1 gallon (gal.) = 4.546 l
1 US gallon   = 3.785 l

1 cm^3 = 0.061 cubic inch
1 m^3 = 35.315 cubic feet

1 litre (l) = 1.76 pints
1 litre (l) = 0.22 gallons

Mass:

1 ounce (oz) = 28.3495 g
1 pound (lb) = 0.453 kg
1 ton (t)   = 1016 kg

Temperature:

Degrees Celsius	Degrees Fahrenheit
− 17.8 °C	= 0 °F
− 12.2 °C	= 10 °F
− 6.7 °C	= 20 °F
− 1.1 °C	= 30 °F
0 °C	= 32 °F
4.4 °C	= 40 °F
10 °C	= 50 °F
20 °C	= 68 °F
30 °C	= 86 °F
40 °C	= 104 °F
50 °C	= 122 °F

Other units:

degrees kelvin (°K)
1 °K = 1 °C/1.8 °F
Absolute zero = −273.15 °C

Energy:

   1 joule   = 0.2388 calories (cal)
1000 joules   = 0.9478 Btu
   1 cal   = 4.1868 joules
   1 Btu   = 1055.06 joule

(Btu = British thermal unit)